Life, Memories and Faith

Poems About The Pain Of People That Lost Their Loved Ones And About Life That Is Precious

M.J. ZITNANSKY

ISBN 978-1-950818-70-9 (paperback)

Copyright © 2020 by M.J. Zitnansky

All rights reserved. No part of this publication may be reproduced, distributed, or transmitted in any form or by any means, including photocopying, recording, or other electronic or mechanical methods without the prior written permission of the publisher. For permission requests, solicit the publisher via the address below.

Rushmore Press LLC
1 888 733 9607
www.rushmorepress.com

Printed in the United States of America

Contents

On Remembrance Day 7
We Remember 8
The Dying Soldier and the Raven 9
Going to War 10
Don't Miss Me for Long 11
The Life's Journey 12
Your Loved One is Dying 13
At the Autumn of Your Life 14
Strive to be Happy 15
The Friend Who Just Stands By 16
On Death 17
The Husband to His Wife 18
When the New Day Started 19
I Wish You Would Not Cry 20
Being Lonely 21
On Getting Old 22
The Loss of a Friend 23
If You Lose a Loved One 24
The Memories 25
On Love 26
At the End of Life's Journey 27
She Left You Here 28
Life's Sorrow 29
To Be or Not to Be 30
The Desire 31
Love and Pain 32
The Love is Never in Vain 33
On Love That Never Ends 34
The Time is Going 35
There is No One to Wipe off My Tear 36
Losing a Loved One 37

On Forgiveness	38
Falling in Love	39
Stand By Me	40
I Remember	41
A Road to Home	42
I See You in My Mind	43
The Journey Back	44
I Want to Know	45
The Wish	46
At Tamagami Wilderness	47
The Storm	48
We Need a Mediator	50
You Will Tell Me	51
I Need Peace	52
To Live	53
The Northern Lights	54
The Moonlight	55
Two Lights in the Dark	56
My Grandchildren	57
The Christmas Bells	58
The Day When it All Began	59
You Are the One	60
Snares of Evil	61
The Life That Will Last	62
What is Wrong and What is Right	63
The Longing	64
The Master's Artistry	65
God is Real	66
The Designer	67
The Search	68
We Have a Role to Play	69
The Prayer for Guidance	70
The Thanks	71

The War on God 72
The Confusion 73
Katelyn..74
The Spring 75
The Summer 76
The Fall..77
The Winter 78
The Chimpanzees..79
The Bird's Migration 80
The Dying Mother 81
The Quest 82
Rich and Poor 83
The Secret Places in the Woods 84
When the Troubles Come Your Way.................................85
The Old Steps in Prague...86
The Rain 87
The Little Lake...88
My Duty to Tell 89
The Transcendence...91
The Tree 92
The Dishonest Agent 93
The Tree That is Loved..94
The Dream..95
The Neighbour's Help 96
The Lost Love 97
Abide By Me 98

On Remembrance Day

On Remembrance Day
We cry for you who died for us,
Who died for us so we can live,
Who died on the fields, in ruins and in broken glass.

You died among the poppy seeds,
In cities, on hills and in mud,
You died on the fruitless fields,
Away from those whom you loved.

We can't thank you enough,
We can just honour you more
For what you have done
And show you, that you are not alone.

People are still fighting,
There is still a lot of cry,
Soldiers are still dying
In countries near and far.

We have to find out how to stop the wars,
We have to find out how to live in peace,
How to make our future bright,
We have to find out what to have peace needs.

We Remember

We remember you who did not survive.
We remember you who were sent to fight
At home and in foreign lands,
Against the enemies and their might.

There are still those who want to fight.
Our future is still not bright.
The enemy is forcing us to strike,
With our soldiers losing life.

Our soldiers that fell once had a life,
They were loving and they were loved.
They had mothers, girlfriends, children and wives,
But by bullets and grenades they have died.

Who will stop those who want to fight,
Those who want to conquer us with their might,
Who will bring the torch with light
And order them to stop the fight.

Innocent soldiers, mother's sons,
Fathers, husbands, lovers died,
In countries far away,
Far away from those whom they loved.

The Dying Soldier and the Raven

It was like thunder and lightning
All around.
Then I was shot
And fell to the ground.

I wanted to get up and go,
But I could not move.
My body failed me,
I knew I was doomed.

Then I saw a maiden
All dressed in white.
She had a halo,
Was she my bride?

She was walking on a meadow,
She came to me,
She gave me her hand
And took me under a tree.

We lay under a tree
And she gave me a kiss.
The kiss that she gave me
Brought me back like a bliss.

I realized that I was hit.
I realized that I would die
And when I opened my eyes,
The last thing I saw was a raven's eye.

Going to War

"Don't go to the war my son.
Don't go, stay with me."
"I have to go my dearest mother,
I have to go, it is my destiny."

"I am afraid I won't see you again.
I am afraid you won't come back."
"I will come back my dearest mother.
Wait for me and look ahead."

The son left, the mother was crying,
The son promised that he would write.
The mother prayed, the mother hoped,
The son was writing that there is no fight.

The mother missed him every day,
Checking the mailbox and waiting for the mail.
The son was writing that he had fun,
He wrote that he would sail away.

He wrote that he would go far away
That his ship would not stay.
The mother was worried,
She was crying every day.

The son wrote a letter before he left.
He was excited about the life ahead.
The mother was waiting, hoping he would write,
But no mail came, just the telegram was sent.

The enemy struck the ship that was sent.
There is no grave where it should be,
The mother is crying,
Her son is buried in the sea.

Don't Miss Me for Long

I was shot and I will die
There is no help around.
I know that you will cry for me
When you will find out.

I wish so much you would not cry,
But I can't have it my way,
You will think of the many things
We could not say.

When you will find out that I have died
And the sun was set for me,
I want you to remember
Not to cry for a soul set free.

There were so many duties I had to do,
There was no escape.
I thank you for the strength you gave me
By loving me and promising your hand.

I know you love me and I love you,
Miss me, but don't miss me for long.
There is a new life you have to live,
There is another man to whom you will belong.

The Life's Journey

Everybody has a life's journey
That he calls his own.
Everybody has a journey
That he walks alone.

Even if life's spring time
Is happy to recall,
Some times in our life
Are not happy at all.

During the life's journey
We will laugh and cry,
We will be hurt and happy,
Our friends will stop to say goodbye.

Even if life's journey
Is nice to recall,
The autumn of our life
Is the nicest of all.

When all the problems of our life
Will gradually disappear,
Our hearts will be filled
With peace and good will.

Your Loved One is Dying

Your beloved is dying,
You have to be with her to see her go!
But by seeing that,
Your pain will only grow.

If you will not be there
To see your beloved go,
Your love will still be with her
And your love for her will show.

If your beloved will die without you,
You will sit down and cry,
But her spirit will be with you,
She will help you to live, she will try.

If your beloved will die without you,
She will receive help from above,
You don't have to worry about her,
Her soul will still sense your love.

At the Autumn of Your Life

When your years near the past
Gently surrender to things of youth.
In the autumn of your life
There is more knowledge and more truth.

The pace grows slower
And you will become less restless too.
Your heart will be more gentle
And remember the joys it once knew.

Hold fast to dreams,
Don't let them die.
Cherish your friends
That will stand by.

Be cheerful and try to be happy,
But if sadness makes you cry,
Surrender, but not for long,
Remember that to be happy is worth the try.

When your youthful yearning
Will gradually cease,
The rest of your life
Will be filled with love and peace.

Strive to be Happy

The world is full of drudgery and sadness.
There is a lot of confusion in life,
But we have to keep peace in our souls
To be able to achieve happiness for which we strive.

The happiness is a promise from above.
We can achieve it if we strive.
We have to be cheerful and trust
In the power which comes to us with love.

We were told that love is precious,
But life tells us that it is not real.
Many people can feign affection
Can be dishonest and destroy the love you feel.

Try to keep the strength of spirit
The misfortunes in life are real,
You need the shield of strong spirit
And your happiness will be near.

Look at the marvels of nature.
We live in a beautiful world.
This gives us a good feeling to nurture
Which can keep us content and glad.

The Friend Who Just Stands By

There is a lot of wisdom
In what we all know
That to have a friend in sorrow
Will make your love for him to grow.

To have a friend in sorrow
Can bring you peace, he can try.
And even if he can do nothing,
You will love the friend who will stand by.

If the friend can't smooth the road
And can't soothe the pain,
If the problem is your own,
The love of friend will stay the same.

In the time of sorrow
If there is nothing the friend can do,
It will bring you consolation
If he will just be with you.

Some troubles are only our own.
The friend can't help us, but he will try.
The friend's love will bring you hope,
Even if the friend will just stand by.

On Death

Death is brutal, to accept it is hard.
It tears us away from all we love,
It tells us to go
And leave everything behind.

There is a place, our destination
Where we all have to go,
A place where we will see our departed loved ones,
Where trees, grass, and flowers grow.

We should not be discouraged
If we will be told to go.
We should feel encouraged
To see the new life with the Heaven's glow.

The Husband to His Wife

When the new day starts without me
I want you to understand,
That the angel came
And took me by the hand.

I had to go where he took me,
To a place far above
And I had to leave on Earth,
The people I truly love.

I don't want you to worry about me,
I am in good hands.
Look after those I left behind,
Be with them when their life ends.

Remember that I will be with you
In good times and in bad,
Each time you will think of me
I can go to you, God said.

So when I am not with you tomorrow
I will still be in your heart.
I know your heart is full of sorrow,
But we don't have to part.

You can think of me, you can talk to me
I will understand.
We will be together again
In the end.

When the New Day Started

When the new day started without you,
I could not understand.
I thought I couldn't live without you,
I thought my life would have to end.

I wish I could realize
That a new life started that day,
And I wish I would not cry
The way I cried that day.

I know that you love me
The same as I love you,
But you left an empty space!
I know you miss me too.

We had so much to live for
So much was left to do!
My head was full of thoughts.
I wanted to talk to you.

You left me and did not say where you went
Or if you would come back for me.
The emptiness and sense of loss
Joined with my heart's agony.

The years are passing,
The time is going,
But my pain is still the same.
If I think about you, I cry
The same as I did that day.

I Wish You Would Not Cry

I was just passing through the Heaven's gate
When I saw you cry.
I thought about the love we shared
And decided to stand by.

I don't want you to cry so much,
Not today nor tomorrow,
Because each time you cry,
Your soul is full of sorrow.

I wish you would not cry,
Because we are not far apart.
Each time you will think of me
I will be in your heart.

I will be with you in memories
Each time you will think of me,
I want you to know that I had to go
To set my soul free.

I did not want to leave you alone,
But it was God's plan.
He wanted me to be with him.
I will be with you in memories again.

I want so much that you would not cry
And know that I had to go,
That an angel came and took my hand
And brought me to my new home.

Being Lonely

When loneliness invades your heart
And you feel all alone,
Then think of those whom you have loved
And go to the place that you call home.

Bury your mind in happy thoughts,
Happy thoughts that you can trust.
Happy thoughts are always with us,
Happy thoughts are those which inspire us.

Your memories are always with you,
Happy thoughts are always near.
You should always remember whose love you shared
Even if it can bring you a silent tear.

God in his gentle
And always loving care
Will let you to remember
The love and joy that once were there.

All that you experienced
On the way to pleasure,
Will stay in your mind
And will bring you memories to treasure.

With happy memories
The loneliness will cease
And your heart will be filled
With happiness and peace.

On Getting Old

When you get old and feeble
Then you should understand,
That you life is not yet over
That it is not yet the end.

The pace gets slower,
The life more serene
And the past that you envision
Will seem like a dream.

The gay days are over,
New time will come in,
There is a new life for you
Which did not yet begin.

Your soul becomes restless
And it becomes keen
To envision what your eyes
Have not yet seen.

When you get old and feeble
You should understand
That you should live your life fully
And your life will stay content.

When the day comes
And your life will cease
You will live a new life
Full of beauty and peace.

The Loss of a Friend

When you lose a friend
You try to remember
The joys of that friendship
Even if your heart will tremble.

By losing a friend
Your heart will hurt,
But you have to recover
And go ahead.

During our lifetime
Friends come and go
For friends are a part
Of whom here on Earth we have known.

Even if joys of friendship
Are nice to remember,
To the loss of a friend
Is hard to surrender.

Friendship is precious,
But be on guard.
If you lose your friend,
Try not to lose your heart.

If You Lose a Loved One

If you lose a loved one
Keep him in your mind.
If you lose a loved one,
The memories stay behind.

Keep these memories as treasure,
Never let them go,
Think about him with pleasure,
It will let your love for him grow.

Our loved ones will change the dwelling place,
We have to let them go.
They will wait for us in the universe,
They are not dead even six feet below.

We can cry and be sad for a while,
But we can't forget about the life here on Earth.
The pain we feel is a trial,
It makes us stronger to be able to follow them to the universe.

The Memories

Thinking of our loved ones
Whom we loved and lost,
Makes us to remember,
But causes pain the most.

Remembering is proper,
We should remember and honour them
By doing so we will bring back the memories,
But their passing is not us to blame.

Their souls are in eternity and free
Free of worries and of pain.
They are with us in memories,
But memories and life are not the same.

Some memories can bring us laughter,
Some memories can bring the pain,
Some memories can bring us tears,
The memories help us to see our loved ones in our mind again.

The memories are important
For those we loved and for us.
They bring us closer to eternity,
They are renewing our past.

On Love

When we will be at the end of our journey
And our life will be called the past,
We will remember people we loved,
We will remember the life that went so fast.

We should know that love lasts forever,
That it comes with us to eternity,
That the love from the past starts anew
And will always set us free.

Because the love never dies,
It can be felt here on Earth.
It can be sent by those we dearly loved
And whose lives we have shared.

We don't have to worry about our love tomorrow
When our life will be called the past,
Because our love will survive,
Because our love will always last.

At the End of Life's Journey

When our life gets slower
And our mind more serene,
We like to envision
What we have not yet seen.

While the life's primetime
We like to recall
The serene time of our life
Is the best time of all.

When we come to the end of life's journey
We like to recall
The time when we were young
From most times of all.

When our heart will become less restless
Our life will become more peaceful too
And our heart will envision
The joys it once knew.

Our heart will envision
Our youthful time of joy and pleasure
And it will become a memory
That we will keep as treasure.

When we come to the end of life's journey
We should understand
That everybody walks this journey
And that it is not time when our life will end.

She Left You Here

By hearing about your loved one
I know how you feel.
The end of your plans.
The end of your dreams.

Your darling was taken away from you.
Your soulmate left you here.
Your heart is broken,
You wish she would be near.

You feel lonely and betrayed.
How can you enjoy your life
If the one who left you
Was supposed to be your wife?

You go to places where you have been together,
You whisper for her to hear,
It brings your memories together,
With love and a silent tear.

There is life where she has gone,
But you can still sense her here,
Her love is still with you,
Which can wipe off your tear.

You will never forget her,
But you are young and need a new life.
She will always love you,
She knows you need a wife.

Life's Sorrow

It should bring you a comfort
That sorrow, grief and pain
Are a part of living,
Even if you are youthful and a flame.

Through the depth of sorrow
You will appreciate love,
Will cherish memories of joy
And understand life.

Everybody has a sorrow
Sometimes in his life,
But it is not a reason
Not to try to strive.

It should be your comfort
That sorrow, pain and woe
Are a part of your life
To help your soul to grow.

When you grow old
And saw what you could have seen,
You will look at your life
And think that it was like a dream.

To Be or Not to Be

To be or not to be?
We all ask this question.
Life is full of problems
We have no protection.

Life is full of snare of evil,
We have to try to conquer them.
We wait for gifts from Heaven
And hope to be protected by them.

To be or not to be?
That is what we ask.
We look for answers,
Answers that can't be found.

If we want to be and live,
We have to take what life will bring,
Loads of misfortunes and troubles,
With happy times that luck can swing.

If we decide not to be,
We have to dread of the unknown land,
We have to know that it is our destination
And that it is not where our troubles end.

The Desire

Your life is your own,
Don't let anybody your life to disown.
Keep peace in your soul.
You will come to God alone.

Be yourself.
You are unique in the universe.
You have the right to be you
And not to be someone else.

Remember the silence
When dealing with a person who is loud.
Speak your truth clearly
And it will let him to part.

Be gentle to yourself.
Don't distress yourself with dark imagination.
Try to find good people.
There are good people in every nation.

With passing time,
Surrender to your youth.
Be at peace with God
And the happiness will be yours.

Love and Pain

Love is patient, love is kind, but it can be painful
If you already tried
To win that love
And now you are apart.

Love doesn't mean
To win the heart of the one you love.
It is what you feel within
That makes you happy and strive.

Love makes you humble
Love puts your own interests aside.
Love can be painful.
Love and pain walk side by side.

The Love is Never in Vain

When we met
I knew you and you knew me.
When we fell in love
I loved you and you loved me.

Nobody asked us
If this is true or how it should be.
Love has to be noticed,
Love has to shine from you and from me.

You were patient, you were kind,
I was trusting, even if I would weep.
Love is not for sale
It is only for keep.

I was enduring the things that went wrong;
You were building a smooth path.
You were my fortress,
You were the one I could trust.

I believed all you said,
You were full of strength and faith.
I loved the life you shared with me,
I learned that love never ends.

I was trusting when I was scared
If the days were not the same.
I learned many things, but I knew
That we did not love in vain.

On Love That Never Ends

Since I was twenty-four
You were always on my side.
You became my teacher,
You became my guide.

I feel lonely and scared without you,
It was hard to let you go.
I think of you everyday
And feel my love to grow.

When will this love stop growing?
There is no more space to grow.
My heart is full of that love,
I love you with all my soul.

If you would be here with me
I could understand,
But you are far away
Which should mean the end.

There is no end for what I feel,
There is no end for my love.
There is no end for what you mean to me,
But I need the peace for which I strive.

Nobody knows how much I love you
And nobody can understand
That my love for you is never ending,
That it did not stop when you left.

When I die I will be beside you
In the tomb that waits for me.
We will rest side by side,
We will be together again, you and me.

The Time is Going

The time is going, the years are passing,
You are still on my mind.
I see you young and healthy,
I see you on my side.

The life with you is a story
That is filled with respect and love.
It's a story about two souls
That cannot stay apart.

Our souls are still connected
With love that never dies.
I can still see you in my mind,
But I can't see you with my eyes.

You are still here with me,
You dry my eyes when I cry,
I see you smiling in my mind,
I know that it was not a goodbye.

There is No One to Wipe off My Tear

My love for you is everlasting,
I always remember that,
But each time tomorrow starts without you
I don't understand.

We had so much to live for,
So much we liked to do,
So much we did not get to say,
So much I wanted to do for you.

When the new day starts without you,
You are always on my mind.
I know I lost my teacher
I know I lost you by my side.

When I think about the life we had together
All the joy and fun we knew,
All that becomes but a memory
Each time I think of you.

I love you and I miss you,
But in memory you are always near.
You are loved and remembered,
But there is no one to wipe off my tear.

Losing a Loved One

Since the time I met you
You were there as my guide.
I will never forget you,
I sense you from the other side.

When you were taken away from me
I could not sleep in the night.
My nights were full of nightmares,
My days were full of fright.

You were always with me,
You tried to calm me down.
I know that you wanted to help me,
You showed me what had to be done.

You showed me the light
In the darkest nights.
You showed me the way to go,
You showed me the Heaven's heights.

The pain of losing a loved one
Is always more or less the same,
But I lost what I lived for.
Can you imagine the pain?

On Forgiveness

To forgive your friend is not easy,
But to forget is a plot.
You can forgive even with your heart bleeding,
To forget you need your soul's accord.

To forgive is the heart's action,
To forget is not the same.
You can forgive and get your peace,
To forget haunts you again and again.

There are people who like hurting.
Their emotions are not the same.
They like to cause pain and disaster.
For them hurting is a game.

Nature tells us to take revenge
The soul tells us to forgive
Nature tells us to get even
The soul tells us to make peace.

Falling in Love

Don't fake love
If it is not real.
Don't pretend
What you don't feel.

Love is precious
If it can be found.
It is hard to find it.
There is not enough love around.

Even if the love can stay forever
You can lose your love.
If your love would disgrace you,
It would be rejected by your heart.

Your heart can reject your love
If it feels it is not real,
If your heart knows
That it is not real what you claim to feel.

Many people lose their love
If their loved one betrays them,
If their love has been mocked,
Than the love will leave them.

Be careful with whom you fall in love
With whom your heart has affection,
With whom you don't want to part,
With whom your love will stay in connection.

Stand By Me

When I grow old and be feeble,
I want you to stand by me.
I hope you will come and say
"I want you to share your life with me."

Because your soul and mine
Are not that far apart,
Each time I think of you
I feel you on my side.

I can think of all we shared,
But I can't think of tomorrow,
Because if I do
My heart is filled with sorrow.

I can talk to you and tell you
How much you are loved
By those who knew you,
You were the one they could trust.

You are loved and remembered
As much as you can be.
I am sure you know about it,
It is the love that you can see.

I Remember

When I visit places
Where you and I have been,
I look around and remember
Which part of it you have also seen.

When I visit those places
My thoughts are very clear.
I know that where I am now,
You once have also been.

I don't want to admit
That I won't always be here,
That I have to take the journey
To a place where you are now my dear.

It is hard to think about
That one day I won't be near.
I don't want to think about it,
But I know that one day I will not be seen.

A Road to Home

When you came to the end of your life,
You told me that you had to go.
You told me I could cry for you,
But not with the head bowed low.

You knew that I will miss you
You told me that my life will change.
I told you that we will see each other again
I saw a smile on your face.

You suffered a lot and wanted to die,
You wanted to be free.
You wanted to go to Heaven.
I thought you forgot about me!

You said that you have to go on a journey,
That each one must go alone.
On a journey of a soul set free,
On the road to home.

I See You in My Mind

When I wake up I think of you
At the time of sunrise's charm.
The same as I enjoy the sun's rays
I enjoy your sole's balm.

The pain you caused when you left me
Is still the same as it was then.
I long for your smile and your courage
The life without you is not the same.

The time is going, the years are passing,
But my soul can't be to blame
That I can't forget about you,
That there are memories to claim.

Those memories are cherished by my soul;
Those memories are there to stay.
I see you in my mind,
In my mind you are still the same.

The Journey Back

When I take the journey back,
Back in time,
I come to the place
Where it all began.

I see you healthy,
I see you young,
I see your eyes
Lit with a spark.

Spark of excitement, spark of love.
You wanted to see everything.
The trees, flowers, lakes,
You liked it all, every little thing.

You liked all that you could have,
You liked to plan and look ahead
And when you died,
You showed me that your life did not end.

You showed me that you did not die,
That you were only transferred
Into another life.
The life that will never end.

I Want to Know

The cottage is still there for you to see.
The cottage life is what you liked.
It is the place where you talked to me.
It is the place where you left memories behind.

The cottage is the place where I think of you with pleasure.
I go to places which you have known,
But the pain that you are not with me has no measure.
I long for you, my love for you has grown.

Do you still listen to the songs of birds we listened together?
Do you still watch the sunset glow
And then disappear at the sunset's closure?
Do you watch your cedars grow?

There are many questions I want to ask you.
There are many things I want to know.
There are many things I want to do for you.
There are deeds that I want to show.

The Wish

The simple life at the cottage was what you liked.
You were always up at a dawn.
You liked to watch the sun to rise
And a new day to be born.

I could not get up so early
I did not want to see the dawn.
You went into your boat
And when I woke up, you were already gone.

I felt lonely without you
I went to the lake to see your boat.
You were far away,
I could only see the ducks float.

You came home with a fish and you were happy.
I could never understand why you liked to fish.
For me fishing was too boring,
For you fishing would satisfy your wish.

At Tamagami Wilderness

At Tamagami wilderness
Where you and I used to go,
I followed you from behind,
You were the one who led the show.

At Tamagami wilderness
You went away in your fishing boat,
You wanted to explore the fishing grounds
And I was put at the island on hold.

I knew bad weather was coming
I did not want you to go,
I wanted you to stay with me.
I did not want to be alone.

I was sitting in the tent
And praying for you to come back.
The waves were big and the lightning came,
I did not know where you went.

It started to rain and it got dark when I heard your boat.
I felt my hope to grow.
You did not get lost, you came back!
The thunder brought you home.

The Storm

It was a dark and stormy time
At the northern wilderness.
You and I were at the island,
But you had no peace.

You wanted to go fishing,
I told you not to go.
You did not have any patience,
You said the fish are biting when the winds blow.

I could not hold you,
You did not want to obey.
You wanted to be free,
You were on your way.

I saw the storm was coming,
I saw your boat go so far.
It should not be me whom God would be blaming
If you would not see your lucky star.

It got dark and windy,
The waves were very high.
I was frightened and I was crying,
The lightning was shining in the sky.

I was praying to God
To bring you back to me,
To save your boat and you
And let your eyes to see.

My mind was in a horror,
I did not know what to do.
The thunder and lightning came closer,
I was standing at the lakeshore, praying to God for you.

I could not believe my ears
When I heard the sound of your boat,
My eyes were full of tears,
I send thanks for you to God.

We Need a Mediator

You were the one who was healing people,
You were the one who knew their pain,
You were the doctor who was helping,
We want you to heal us again.

There are many people here who miss you.
There are many people who have the pain.
We want you to help us
And then the pain will not be the same.

Show us your healing power.
Intervene in Heaven for us here.
Ask God if you could help us,
Show us that you are near.

People are ailing.
People are suffering a lot.
People need a mediator,
Who will plead for them to God.

We know that you are happy,
That finally you are free,
But we all miss you
And you are adored by me.

You Will Tell Me

When I die I'll come to you,
But you have to wait a while.
When I come I'll knock on your door
And I want to see you smile.

When I come I know you will say
That you did not want to die,
That the angel took your hand
And brought you through the sky.

You will tell me that your new place
Was ready far above,
That you did not want to leave behind
Those whom you truly loved.

You will tell me that you missed me
The same as I missed you,
You will tell me that my life on Earth is passed
And my life will start anew.

You will show me your new place
And ask me to stay.
We will continue the love we shared
And live a new life again.

I Need Peace

You heard me crying,
I was not able to sleep.
You heard me crying
Even when the void was so deep.

I hoped to rest my soul
By seeing what once you have seen.
I tried to calm my soul
By going to places where once you have also been.

My soul is longing for you
And can't rest.
My soul is longing for you
And that pains my breast.

I need peace to do my work.
My work is a quest.
I need to find the truth
And when I find it, then I can rest.

To Live

"Live" was the word you said
When I was in agony.
"Live again" will be the words
You will say when you will come back for me.

The time is passing fast
Without me to realize that I should live.
Without me knowing
What kind of meaning to the word "Live" to give.

There is a purpose
For all of us in this world.
The word "Live" has a meaning
For which we all should look ahead.

If we all will look ahead
And search for the meaning of this word,
The world will be a better place
And the meaning of the word "Live" will be shared.

The Northern Lights

On one night, a silent night,
When creatures and nature sleep
You woke me up: "Get up and see,
The northern lights, the lights above the trees!"

What a sight it was to see
Those lights when the nature sleeps,
They came up in the darkest night
Dancing above the trees.

I wish everybody could see those lights,
How they are dancing on the skies,
Coming to us from the northern pole
During the darkest summer nights.

Those lights are brighter than the stars,
The clouds let them flow,
Dancing above the tops of trees,
Making the skies glow.

The Moonlight

When I was sitting at the lake one night,
I imagined you were with me.
I put my head on your shoulder,
You were again close to me.

The air was calm and the moon was high,
The lake reflected the moon's light,
I was happy, I did not cry,
The stars were shining bright.

I was telling you how much I loved you,
I could not hear you to tell the same,
But I could hear the waves splashing
Against the shoreline again and again.

I was trying to sing a song for you,
The loon was singing in accord,
Then I realized that you are not with me.
The moonlight got very cold.

Two Lights in the Dark

It was night and dark in the woods,
But there were two lights that we have seen.
The lights were still and then they were moving,
Those were not lights as it would seem.

There was life behind those lights
Predator's eyes shining bright,
In the darkness of the woods,
Showing us the wild life's might.

We could not see what is behind those eyes,
But we could see that they meant fight,
Shining in the dark of night,
Releasing in us the hiding fright.

We stayed still and were frightened,
We did not know what to do.
The lights came closer, I was shaking,
I closed my eyes and clung to you.

You let out a roaring sound,
The lights jumped and fled.
I stopped shaking and was happy,
We went back wondering what made us so scared.

My Grandchildren

My husband, you showed us
That God is the one
Who is in Heaven
And whose wish should be done.

God wants us to know
That Heaven exists.
I know in my heart
That this is his wish.

When I think of you my husband
I feel my love to grow,
I see you
Wherever I go.

I see your charming smile,
I see your eyes
Looking at me
In my sleepless nights.

When I think of you
I feel a sorrow, that you could not see
The little darlings
That belong to you and me.

When I think of Heaven
And what you showed to us,
Then I know that you can also see
Those little darlings that belong to both of us.

The Christmas Bells

Winter will bring the Christmas bells
For the child that was born
To the mother in Bethlehem,
Two thousand years ago.

The young mother and her husband
Were travelling alone
When the little child came into this world,
When God's son was born.

The word became flesh on that day
When there was no shelter for the King,
The mother covered him with swaddling cloth,
He had his mother to whom to cling.

The star appeared above the place
Where the little King was born,
The shepherds came to pay their homage,
He was no more alone.

Three kings came from far away,
To greet that little King,
They were guided by the star,
They brought him gold, frankincense and myrrh.

We remember the birth of that little child
At Christmas every year,
Because he came to bring peace and love
For people from far and near.

The Day When it All Began

The day after Christmas
When I sat down
I thought of the day
When it all began.

I thought about the girl
Who early in her teens
Became the mother of our Saviour,
What miracle it means.

I thought about the mother,
What pleasure it must have been
When she saw her child.
When she became a queen.

This queen is now in Heaven
And prays for us.
We are also her children
And she is the mother of all of us.

We should pray to this mother
Who became a queen,
Who can pray for us,
Who can intervene.

You Are the One

Jesus you are the one who told us
That Heaven is for real.
You are the one who showed us
That eternity is not just a dream.

You are the one who showed us
That with love we will grow.
You are the one who reminded us
What the dark force can show.

Dark force causes destruction and despair.
You told us enough about that.
We can't just forgive and forget
Because the dark force will always be a threat.

There is so much despair and sadness
From what the dark force can do.
It causes death and destruction.
We cry for help to you.

We have to get organized and united
To conquer that dark force.
We pray for help and protection
We wonder what is its cause.

You are the one who told us
That Heaven exists.
You are the one who wants us
To live in harmony and peace.

Snares of Evil

You were guiding me through the snares of evil,
My Lord and my God.
You showed me what to do
And how to solve my plot.

There were many snares of evil
That were on my way.
You were guiding me through them
And thanks to you I am good today.

If we would just realize
That God wants to help us and be our guide,
If we would ask for help and protection,
He would reduce our plight.

To believe in God is our salvation,
To believe in God will help us to strive,
To believe in God will reduce our frustration,
To believe in God will finish our fight.

We are heading into the wrong direction
We don't know what is wrong or right.
We are confused and misguided.
Without God's guidance we will not survive.

The Life That Will Last

You are teaching us God,
That you are the one whom we should trust.
You made the Earth and Heaven
And you gave it all to us.

You are showing us God,
That we were made by you.
You gave us wisdom,
We should know what to do.

If we will not listen to your teachings God,
And won't see what you have done,
We will live like people that are blinded
And the proper work on Earth will not be done.

We are stubborn and don't see your power.
We want to imitate you but we sin.
We are destroying each other
And our future will be grim.

God, we know that life on Earth
Finishes with the past,
But you showed us that life with you
Is the one that will always last.

What is Wrong and What is Right

We have known from history
That wickedness brings disaster.
We don't want to witness what is known from history
And to be those whom God will be after.

We don't want to be like Sodom and Gomorrah,
We want to do God's will.
We want to live according to his commandments.
We don't want to sin.

If we will not live according to God's will
How can we be saved?
Only confusion and disaster
Is what we can see ahead.

God wants us to prosper.
He wants us to reign.
He wants us to see what is wrong and right.
He wants his thoughts and our thoughts to be the same.

We have to pray to God for guidance.
We have to pray to him to be helped,
We have to know that he is our designer
And that he wants to see us saved.

The Longing

We are all longing
In that sense we are all the same.
Can we say that we are belonging
To something big that has fame?

We know that we were created
We know that we were made.
This fact can't be disputed
We know that our bodies will fade.

We are smart and want to explain
With science that we are all the same.
We dispute the creator and say
That not creation but science plays the game.

Science can't explain how we became,
Science is silenced if asked to explain.
The steps of evolution, can't explain
How it all began.

Science can't explain the longing.
The longing that is in our hearts,
The longing that is showing
Where science and creation parts.

The Master's Artistry

The sun shines on Earth during the day,
The moon shines on Earth during the night,
The stars are like lanterns shining bright,
God looks at it and says: "It is alright."

Why don't we acknowledge God for what he is?
He is the master who created us.
He gave us all what we need.
He is the master of Earth and the skies.

The beauty of nature is evident,
We admire the beauty of skies, land and seas
We acknowledge their existence,
But we don't take it for what it is.

It is a work of the Creator,
The Creator who wants us to live in peace.
He gave the Earth to us.
We are his masterpiece.

The beauty of flowers, plants and trees
Is evident on all that human eye sees,
But we still don't want to believe
That it is all the designer's deeds.

God shows us his power
He shows us his majesty,
He wants us to know about him,
He shows us his artistry.

God is Real

I have heard about you
From far and near,
I have always known God
That you are real.

I have heard about you God
I know that you exist.
People talk about you God
From west to east.

From north to south
Your deeds are done.
All over the world people praise you.
I know that you are the one.

God don't condemn us, your people
For the sins we have done.
Help us to fight the evil,
Save the souls of people that the enemy has won.

The Designer

God is the designer.
He designed you and me.
God is the designer
Who designed the Heaven, the Earth and the sea.

The scientists are trying to discredit the designer.
They say that creation was by a chance,
Even if we can see the designer's creation
On the very first glance.

The creatures are too complicated
To become and not to be designed.
There were not enough resources
When the creation was timed.

When the scientists see the human body
How the human body was designed,
They become speechless,
They experience a fright.

How can you not see the designer
Who gave you eyes to see!
Doesn't he talk to you
The same as he talks to me?

The Search

The search for God is universal
We all want to find him.
We need his love and protection,
But the search for him is still dim.

The search for God is in our longing
Which is embedded in our hearts
And because of this longing
We hope we have a chance.

We hope that we have a chance
To accomplish our dream,
A dream that one day we will find him
And will be able to be with him.

We Have a Role to Play

To believe in God is essential,
To believe in God should be our aim
Because he is our Creator,
Because we have eternity to claim.

The eternity can be good or bad,
In eternity we will get what we deserved.
We know that there is life after death,
That we have another life ahead.

There is enough testimony
From people that witnessed that.
We should believe in eternity,
We have learned enough what to expect.

Let us be honest,
Let us be good,
Let us help each other,
Let us know that we did what we could.

If we can do good deeds,
There should be no delay,
We should always know
That we have a role to play.

The Prayer for Guidance

There is a quest in my heart
That nobody can see.
There is a quest for you God
When you talk to me.

I will satisfy this quest for you God.
I want you to be known everywhere,
I know that you are using the week
To outshine the strong here and there.

The quest for you God
Is not easy to do,
Therefore God I have to pray for guidance
Everyday to you.

You know God that I will find you.
I want to let people know who you are.
I want to open their minds.
You know God that I will try.

The Thanks

Thank you the Almighty
For guiding my mind,
For helping me in my troubles
And for comforting me in my fright.

Your guidance helps me in my living,
I sense you on my side.
You are always forgiving
And help me in my plight.

In danger and confusion
I hurry to your side.
You are always helping me in crisis
And so you became my guide.

You guide me through dangers,
You know what to do,
How to solve my problems
And that is why I will always pray to you.

The War on God

There is a war on you God.
We crucified your son,
We killed him one day
Because we did not understand what he had done.

You did not punish us God
Because you gave us a free will.
Your son came to open the Heavens
So that our future is not grim.

There is so much in store for us God,
So much that we can't understand.
We live for now,
But don't see the end.

God, people deny that you are the Creator,
They say that creation was by chance.
They don't see the beauty of your creation
Even if it can be seen at first glance.

God, please have patience with us.
We just don't understand.
We have to know more about you
And we will be happy at the end.

We have to learn more about life,
We have to learn that life is not a game,
We have to learn that you are the Creator
And that we have the eternity to gain.

The Confusion

The world is in confusion
What used to be wrong is now okay.
It is no more who we are,
But it is the role that we play.

The roles are confusing.
The nature is no more the same.
Are we hiding our nature
Or are we just playing the game?

We are living a real life.
We are living a life that was designed.
Are we trying to change the God's nature?
Are we bringing on the plight?

We are designed to love each other.
To love each other and not to sin.
By loving each other we celebrate God's nature.
This celebration means to agree with him.

Katelyn

You are the one who was expected.
You are the one I knew would come.
You are a gift from Heaven.
I knew that it would be done.

You are a beautiful little girl
You make us all happy, I can say.
Will you be happy too?
The future is what makes us worried every day.

You are a little girl that always smiles.
Your smile gives us strength day by day.
We need your smile to continue
To go through struggles that we claim.

Will you love me when I will need you?
Will you be there
When I will need you to cross over?
Will you know where?

Dedicated to Katelyn my granddaughter.

The Spring

Sun is shining, sky is bright, indicating a new life
For plants and creatures that were under winter's might.
The birds are singing songs of joy
To be freed of the winter's plight.

The birds are singing, the birds are humming,
The trees are getting a new sap,
Waking them up and helping them grow.
New life is sensed ahead.

The grass is growing, the trees are budding,
It's a pleasure to see it grow.
The fisherman is getting ready
To catch a fish from the lake below.

The bears woke up from their deep sleep,
They watch their cubs where they go,
The ducks are ready to sit on their eggs,
The rabbits cover their little ones with fur from head to toe.

The spring is short, the summer is coming,
Everything is just for grasp.
Nights are shorter, days are longer,
Nature is fulfilling its task.

The Summer

The summer time is a happy time.
The children are happy as they can be.
The adults do all kinds of sports
And go to see the sites they want to see.

Summer time is a happy time
For creatures and people the same.
It gives them nourishment and supplies
For the long winter's game.

God supplies the chlorophyll
For everything to grow.
Chlorophyll is the substance
That scientists are not privileged to know.

Everything fits in its place,
Everybody knows what to do.
Everybody is doing his own thing.
There is no need for ado.

The birds, ducks, loons and geese
Are teaching their little ones to fly,
Preparing them for a big move
Before winter comes and brings snow into the sky.

The bees are zooming around the country
Pollinating all that blooms and grows.
They are helpful to the nature and people,
They are a treasure for us both.

People are busy with all kinds of chores,
But the creatures are busy the most
Because the summer is short and they have a duty
To be prepared for the winter's host.

The Fall

The summer is over,
The fall is here,
Indicating with falling leaves
That the winter is coming near.

The fall's wind is blowing faster,
The fall's frost makes the ground hard.
The fields are bare, there is no pasture
For animals that stayed behind.

Some animals store food for winter,
Some animals fly away
To find the pasture in warm countries
And when they find it, they will stay.

After fall will show us what to do
And puts the bears to a long deep sleep,
It will give us very long nights,
It will give us memories to keep.

There is no time for memories in summer,
The summer makes us go, go, go.
Only fall makes us to remember
The summer by cold and hostile winter's show.

The Winter

The winter is coming,
The bare woods are still,
Waiting for the frosty Heaven
To send the snow to spill.

The snow is falling, spilling snowflakes,
Everything is white as it can be,
It is dispersing the darkness
With snow's pedigree.

The woods changed into white trees,
The fields changed into fields of snow,
The nature is dazzling white,
Changed by the winter's blow.

With snowy hills and frozen lakes
The nature is getting a good sleep,
Before it's waking up in spring time
From the sleep that was so deep.

The Chimpanzees

God, you created a marvel.
You made a man,
But we are disgracing your name.
Again and again.

The men think
That we came from a chimpanzee!
God's master work or chimpanzee?
God, I know that you created me.

To think that our ancestors were the chimpanzees
Offends you God.
We want to know that you are the designer.
Please solve for us this plot.

Why did the chimpanzees not change their image?
Why are the chimpanzees still the same?
Why should we believe we come from the chimpanzees?
Who is playing this game?

People all over the world
Are talking about you God.
They dispute the scientists,
They can see what is and what is not.

God, why did you give the chimpanzees
Twenty four pairs of chromosomes
And only twenty three pairs to us?
Many people start to believe now
That you created us.

The Bird's Migration

I wonder about the bird's migration
I wonder where the ducks, geese, loons and robins go.
How they can find their new home
Before the harsh winter blow.

Their wings are designed by the almighty,
Their brains are a wonder of DNA,
Their order and submission,
Their instinct and memory are the same.

They get together in the fall,
They find their warm destination,
They come back to the same place
They are a part of the same nation.

Their little brains are trusting,
Their little hearts know love,
Their little brains are navigated
From the one who reigns above.

The Dying Mother

The mother is dying,
The children stand by,
The husband is crying,
Is this a goodbye?

The dearest mother,
The dearest wife,
They want to help her,
They already tried.

Nobody can help her,
The death is coming near,
Nobody can save her,
They will lose her, that is what they fear.

Where will you go mother
When you leave us here?
What will you do father
When she won't be near?

We will remember you mother,
We all will be near
When you leave your husband,
You don't have to fear.

The Quest

There is a quest in my heart,
That I don't comprehend.
There is a question in my heart,
That needs to be heard.

My consciousness is telling me,
To do my heart's quest.
It is telling me
To solve my heart's request.

To know the truth is essential.
I want to know what the quest will bring.
I need to see what I will find.
I need to know how I should think.

My quest is a quest for truth.
I need to know what the truth is.
I need to disperse the darkness.
I need to solve the quiz.

The atheists say that God does not exist,
The believers say that he does.
The atheists say that the world became from nothing,
The believers say that God created the world and us.

Rich and Poor

There are rich people
And there are poor.
The rich people try to get richer,
The poor people try to endure.

The rich people, they don't worry
What will happen to me or you.
The poor people in contrary
Have to worry and call God to you.

How can they both see clouds to flow,
How can they both see the sunset glow
If there is no justice between rich and poor,
If rich are high and poor are low.

There should be justice for poor people,
Rich people should help them if they try,
There should be help for poor people,
Rich people should show them how to go by.

If rich people would help the poor,
If they would teach them what to do,
The poor people would learn to live
And they would take care of themselves too.

The Secret Places in the Woods

There are secret places in the woods
Where we can't go you or I.
There are secret places in the woods
With trees that touch the sky.

The deer with fawns live in those woods
Where bears with cubs can go,
Where squirrels and rabbits are running free
And moose are hiding, where tall trees grow.

In those secret places high in the woods
The moss and fern grow
And streams are running down into valleys
And fill the rivers below.

Those secret places in the woods
They are not us to see,
Those secret places in the woods
Don't belong to you or me.

The secret places in the woods
Are lit by the stars
During the night when people sleep,
When the moon is moving across the skies.

In those secret places in the woods
The creatures are moving free,
They sleep in caves, burrows, on branches
Or under a fallen tree.

They don't worry about tomorrow,
They eat what they find and see,
They are happy and know hardships,
But they don't complain to you or me.

When the Troubles Come Your Way

When the troubles come your way,
You expect your friends to come and stay.
You don't want to be alone
With the troubles of your own.

Not many friends will come and stay
Until you will see a better day.
Not many friends will see you cry,
They will come and say goodbye.

The few friends that may stay
You will see in your life again.
Nothing else better calms your cry
Then a friend who will stand by.

The Old Steps in Prague

There are steps that lead so high,
On which we walked you and I.
There are steps where lovers go,
Where you can feel your love grow.

Those steps are there for lovers sake,
Unless you step on them by mistake.
Once you step on those steps,
You will be in love and nothing helps.

Those are the steps where lovers go
If they want their love to grow.
Those steps have power over you,
You won't be the same, you won't be you.

They will enchant you with a lover's charm,
With the charm that can't be undone.
You will never be the same,
You can't be the old you again.

So take care to climb up those old steps
Where people lose their hearts and heads.
Walk up those steps only if you know
That you want your love to grow.

The Rain

It is raining, it is quiet in spring morning.
The Earth is thirsting for the rain
That was postponed again and again.
The Earth is swallowing the raindrops and easing its strain.

The birds are hiding under tree branches
Sheltered from the rain,
Covering their little ones
With their feathers as much as they can.

The little ones peak out their heads
Wondering what is going on,
Why their mother did not bring them
The food to live on.

The rabbits hide in their burrows
Or a hollow fallen tree,
Waiting for the rain to stop
Knowing that new grass will grow as juicy as can be.

The squirrels are hiding in the trees,
They know what is the best,
They spread their long tails,
Sheltering their nest.

The frogs are excited over the rain,
They were worried about their tadpoles.
The tadpoles were struggling in shallow water
They were the ones that needed rain the most.

Everybody seems to be happy
That the rain has finally come,
Because without the rain
Nothing can be done.

The Little Lake

I know about a place
Where little lake is.
The lake is like a jewel
Embedded in the trees.

The trees are like guards
Protecting the lake
From all of those
Who like to take.

The fern is growing around the lake,
The lake is a haven for the fish,
The birds are nesting in the trees
Surrounding the lake for centuries.

Fallen trees found their rest
On the ground or in the lake
And under the fallen trees
Is a home for a snake.

The lake is a secret place
Where beaver has his house
The forest is a sanctuary
Treasured by all of us.

My Duty to Tell

The day started as any day,
But I was sad and felt lonely
At the anniversary of the day you left.
I decided to see you there
At the place where you rest.

It was calm, mild wind was blowing
The sun was shining
At the place where you rest.
I put flowers into the vase
And I made to you a request.

I asked you to let me stay,
I have to be here and to be strong
To be able to fulfill my promise and my duty
That I try to do so long.

My place is waiting for me
Six feet in the ground
It does not take long to be beside your body
I know that it is the place where I belong.

I have a duty here on Earth
To tell people about the place
Where your soul went.
It is my duty and request
To tell people about that event.

I saw you dead
I knew you will go
To the place of no return
Where your soul is living now
The place to which I also turn.

You showed me that you are living again
At the place of no return
You want me to tell people about it
To tell them not to be afraid
That death is not a quit.

The Transcendence

If transcendence would be possible,
You could be visible to me.
I could see you again
And you could talk to me.

Without transcendence
I can see you only in my mind,
I can talk to you still,
But you can't tell me where you could be found.

Without transcendence
Your presence can't be seen,
But your spirit can come still
And be in places where we have been.

One day I will be able to see you again
And you will be real
When God will tell me to come
And that will be the end of my zeal.

The Tree

Tree, tree, tree
Listen to me.
I know you were supposed to fall down,
But who told you to spare me?

It was a nice fall afternoon
When I walked up the hill.
I passed you on the side
When you did someone's will.

I did not disturb you by passing by.
There was no wind. The nature was still.
I was happy to be outside,
One minute later you could kill.

I got inside the cottage
And I saw you fall.
Why did you not fall earlier or later?
Did you answer someone's call?

You were a big, big tree.
If I would walk slower, you could have killed me.
I was shocked by what I had seen.
I know that I was shown that God spared me.

Tree, tree, tree
Why did you not kill me?
I was walking by your side,
One minute later you sent a message to me.

I know that God spared me for a purpose.
What purpose I don't know
I could have died.
Why was I spared? I want God me to show.

The Dishonest Agent

What did you gain by being dishonest?
You were fired, you lost your job!
What did you gain by being greedy?
You lost your good name. It was a fraud.

Your heart is aching,
You created a deceptive plot.
Your brain wanted to do it,
But your heart did not.

You will have to pay for being dishonest,
You will have to pay for being wrong,
You will cry and be sad,
Your desire to correct it will be strong.

How can you correct what you have done?
You lost the trust you have won.
You lost your friends.
They abandoned you one by one.

God will forgive you,
But people will not.
You will have to gain people's trust again.
To gain people's trust will cost you a lot.

The Tree That is Loved

Standing in front of my kitchen window
I see that my tree is loved.
I see the birds jumping from branch to branch
Looking at my tree from above.

The squirrels are chasing each other
Around the trunk of my tree,
When they see me outside,
They look at me.

The cardinal and his spouse
Make a beautiful decoration
For the branches of my tree,
They are the pride of our nation.

Even the raccoon likes to climb up
And sit on the branch.
He also loves my tree
Even if I don't like to give him that chance.

The Dream

I heard the music in my dream.
The music was sounding clear
In midst of colours and lights beam
It felt like heaven was coming near.

The music sounded like celebration.
Celebration of life.
It made me to listen
And think of wishes for which I strive.

I still remember that music
With trumpet sounding high,
I remember the strings of colours
Coming down from the sky.

The colours were rainbow colours
Embedded in silver light.
I remember the colours brightness
Shining in the darkest night.

I wish I knew
What the dream was about.
I don't know what it wants to tell me
I know it showed me the God's might.

The Neighbour's Help

The mother died, the children stayed behind.
For them everything had changed.
They did not want to tell their father
About the sorrow that they shared.

The father was struggling to be helpful,
He was hiding his own pain,
He had to take care of the children
He had many problems, nobody was to blame.

The neighbour knew what had happened,
She lost her partner too.
She knew the pain and sorrow
And she knew what to do.

She brought the food to the children,
She was hiding her own pain.
She came over to the children,
She came again and again.

The children started to be happy,
The father saw that she made no claim.
He started to like her caring
And soon a new family they became.

The Lost Love

The world is full of sorrow,
You have lost your love,
But that should not stop you
To find another life.

Only love that is faithful
Deserves to be called love
Not the love that betrays you
Is worthy to be in your life.

Your life will still be fruitful
When you will find a faithful love
And you will be thankful
To God from above.

Your new love will be stronger
It will prosper in new light
That will shine on you
From the shadow of the doubt.

You will find a true love this time,
It will ignite your heart
And you will be able to love again
And give your love a new start.

Abide By Me

God, when I fail
To be in touch with you,
Abide by me.

God, when I get lost
And search for you,
Abide by me.

God, when I lose my faith
Even just for a short time,
Abide by me.

God, when I get discouraged
To do your work,
Abide by me.

God, when I get ridiculed
And disbelieved,
Abide by me.

God, when it is hard
To do what you want from me,
Abide by me.

God, stay by my side
Each time I doubt
And abide by me.

www.ingramcontent.com/pod-product-compliance
Lightning Source LLC
Chambersburg PA
CBHW030344100526
44592CB00010B/814